RECLAIMING the GROUND

REGIONAL & SPIRITUAL WARFARE STRATEGIES

Ryan LeStrange

Reclaiming the Ground

Copyright © 2021 by Ryan LeStrange

Published by LeStrange Global LLC

Unless otherwise noted, all Scripture quotations are taken from the New American Standard Bible, copyright © 1960, 1962, 1963, 1968, 1971, 1972, 1973, 1975, 1977, 1995 by The Lockman Foundation. Used by permission. www.Lockman.org

Scripture quotations marked AMP are from the Amplified Bible. Copyright © 2015 by The Lockman Foundation. Used by permission. www.Lockman.org

Scripture quotations marked KJV are from the King James Version of the Bible.

Scripture quotations marked MSG are from *The Message: The Bible in Contemporary English*, copyright © 1993, 1994, 1995, 1996, 2000, 2001, 2002. Used by permission of NavPress Publishing Group.

Scripture quotations marked NIV are taken from the Holy Bible, New International Version®, NIV®. Copyright © 1973, 1978, 1984, 2011 by Biblica, Inc.® Used by permission of Zondervan. All rights reserved worldwide. www.zondervan.com. The "NIV" and "New International Version" are trademarks registered in the United States Patent and Trademark Office by Biblica, Inc.®

Scripture quotations marked NKJV are taken from the New King James Version®. Copyright © 1982 by Thomas Nelson. Used by permission. All rights reserved.

Cover Design by J. L. Designs Creative Group

CONTENTS

CHAPTER 1: DISCOVERING GOD'S DREAM	1
CHAPTER 2: LIVING WITH EYES WIDE OPEN	9
CHAPTER 3: DIVINE PARTNERS	25
CHAPTER 4: RECLAIMING GEOGRAPHICAL TERRITORIES	33
CHAPTER 5: TEARING DOWN EVIL ALTARS	49
CHAPTER 6: WORD, WORSHIP, AND PRAYER	71
CHAPTER 7: TENDING YOUR OWN SOIL	89
CHAPTER 8: CONCLUSION	99
NOTES	103

Chapter 1

DISCOVERING GOD'S DREAM

Have you ever stopped to ask yourself what God's dream is for us? What is in the mind of the Lord for a people, a place, or a gathering? What is the thing that He wants to do? What is in His heart? In many ways I view our walk with God as a journey into the unknown. We are extended the privilege of getting to know the Creator of the universe. As we move deeper into His love and into a relationship with Him, we are brought to a pathway of discovery. Layer by layer and bit by bit, He removes the blinders from our eyes that have kept us from our dreams. We may have given up on our dreams because we didn't think them possible, yet somehow, in the midst of His overwhelming love, we discover infinite possibilities. As we grow in confidence of His unfathomable love for us, we are empowered to move beyond the shackles of limited thinking and dreaming, and we are released to embrace a bold new world of possibilities.

> …that He would grant you, according to the riches of His glory, to be strengthened with power through His Spirit in the inner man, so that Christ may dwell in your hearts through faith; and that you, being rooted and grounded in love, may be able to comprehend with all the saints what is the breadth and length and height and depth, and to know the love of Christ which surpasses knowledge, that you may be filled up to all the fullness of God.
> —Ephesians 3:16–19

Every step that we are to take and every plan that the Father has ordained for us have already been declared. Nothing is left to chance.

> Your eyes have seen my unformed substance; and in Your book were all written the days that

were appointed for me, when as yet there was not one of them [even taking shape]. How precious also are Your thoughts to me, O God! How vast is the sum of them! If I could count them, they would outnumber the sand. When I awake, I am still with You.

—Psalm 139:16–18, AMP

The Master Planner has ordained our steps and recorded them. Our privilege is to be able to discover each and every detail that He lovingly crafted for our lives. As we walk with Him in intimacy and trust, He unveils plans and purposes that were established before the foundation of the earth.

Blessed be the God and Father of our Lord Jesus Christ, who has blessed us with every spiritual blessing in the heavenly places in Christ, just as He chose us in Him before the foundation of the world, that we would be holy and blameless before Him.

—Ephesians 1:3–4

His plans and purposes are His dreams for our lives. There are dreams for us individually, dreams for our families, and dreams for people and nations. It is imperative that we live with simple but profound questions in our hearts: God, what have You planned for me? What have You planned for Your people? And what have You planned for this territory?

I often say that the prophetic anointing is the ministry of discovery. The Father opens our eyes and ears so that we may hear and see what He has already declared. We discover what is fact in the unseen realm, and we pull it down by faith into the seen realm. We labor in the realm of invisible mysteries and possibilities in order to change and frame our generation with God's plan and power.

THY KINGDOM COME

I will never forget a life-changing encounter I had with the Lord a number of years ago. I had just finished preaching in a small church in the mountains of rural Virginia and was headed home. At the time, I was living in Tennessee and working for my spiritual father, Dr. Norvel Hayes. I had a Bible college student with me, and as we were driving, I suddenly felt a deep unction for the territory we were driving through, which was right on the border of Southwest Virginia and Northeast Tennessee. As we came through the area, I had a sudden unction to begin to pray. We left our route and took a detour. God's presence overwhelmed me as we drove through that region, and my heart swelled with compassion and sense of destiny. As quickly as that burden came, it also left.

I knew no one in that area. I had no idea why God burdened me like that. I know now that He was inviting me into His dream for a people and a place. Years later God sent me into that same territory to plant a church. I knew one person, and we began meetings in her house. The Lord was taking me on a great adventure. He was inviting me into His dream. The prayer was a glimpse of what was to come.

When teaching His disciples to pray, Jesus said:

> After this manner therefore pray ye: Our Father which art in heaven, hallowed be thy name. Thy kingdom come, thy will be done in earth, as it is in heaven.
> —Matthew 6:9–10, KJV

Jesus was imploring His followers to pray with distinct vision. He was instructing us to pray for the kingdom of God to be in such operation on earth that heaven breaks forth here and now. Before you freak out and think I am saying something crazy, let me be clear: I know that there is a place called heaven where born-again people will go, where the presence of

God infuses the atmosphere, and where death is no more. It is a place where the river of life flows freely, knowledge is infinite, and pain is not present.

> Then he showed me a river of the water of life, clear as crystal, coming from the throne of God and of the Lamb, in the middle of its street. On either side of the river was the tree of life, bearing twelve kinds of fruit, yielding its fruit every month; and the leaves of the tree were for the healing of the nations. There will no longer be any curse; and the throne of God and of the Lamb will be in it, and His bond-servants will serve Him; they will see His face, and His name will be on their foreheads. And there will no longer be any night; and they will not have need of the light of a lamp nor the light of the sun, because the Lord God will illumine them; and they will reign forever and ever.
> —Revelation 22:1–5

I realize there is an actual heaven where the throne of God is, but I also believe that when Jesus taught His disciples to pray, He was giving us a glimpse of His dream for humanity. He was revealing to us that we could dare to dream of heaven's atmosphere hosted right here. Let's look at Matthew 6:9–10 in *The Message*:

> With a God like this loving you, you can pray very simply. Like this: Our Father in heaven, reveal who you are. Set the world right; do what's best—as above, so below.

What if we believed for something far beyond just a nice Christian life? What if we dreamed with God for heaven on earth? What if we believed for the reality of the kingdom of God in our midst, defeating the works of sickness and disease? After all, there is no cancer in heaven. There are no viruses in heaven. Heaven exudes the life of God.

As it is above, so it should be below! This is the mandate of the church: to occupy territories and establish the kingdom of God until the King shows up and moves in our midst. I am not just talking about a gathering but a lifestyle of heaven on earth. An often-overlooked dimension of the mandate of believers is to govern and legislate. We are to establish the rule of the King on earth in our daily affairs. We are to believe God for people and places. We are to believe God for lives that reflect His glory.

When the King is moving in our midst, heaven is breaking forth. It is below as it is above.

> At evening, when the sun had set, they brought to Him all who were sick and those who were demon-possessed. And the whole city was gathered together at the door. Then He healed many who were sick with various diseases, and cast out many demons; and He did not allow the demons to speak, because they knew Him.
> —Mark 1:32–34, NKJV

These verses are a picture of what the presence of God does on earth. His presence eradicates disease and bondage. His glorious freedom crushes the power of hell and causes demons to leave. We refer to this as revival, but I am becoming increasingly convinced it is the kingdom in operation. Don't get me wrong—I love revival. But I have come to realize that for those who host the King, the reward is the kingdom. When the kingdom is in operation, miracles abound.

This is something much greater than what we learned in our Sunday school classrooms about nice Jesus. This is city-shaking Jesus. This is nation-awakening Jesus. The church is to be His body, alive and active in earth. The question is, *What is the church's mandate?*

Chapter 2

LIVING WITH EYES WIDE OPEN

When the Apostle Paul wrote to the church in Ephesus, he opened his letter by talking about the spiritual blessings of those who have been adopted as sons and daughters by Jesus Christ to Himself. As sons and daughters of the Most High, we are blessed, we are chosen, we are loved, we are accepted, we are redeemed, we are forgiven, and we have the abundant riches of His grace (Eph. 1:3–7). Paul also shared what he was praying for the Ephesian church:

> …the eyes of your understanding being enlightened; that you may know what is the hope of His calling, what are the riches of the glory of His inheritance in the saints, and what is the exceeding greatness of His power toward us who believe, according to the working of His mighty power which He worked in Christ when He raised Him from the dead and seated Him at His right hand in the heavenly places, far above all principality and power and might and dominion, and every name that is named, not only in this age but also in that which is to come. And He put all things under His feet, and gave Him to be head over all things to the church, which is His body, the fullness of Him who fills all in all.
>
> —Ephesians 1:18–23, NKJV

The Apostle Paul was speaking of opening the eyes of the people of God. He was decreeing spiritual sight and prophetic vision. This book began by asking what God's dream is for people and places. In many ways knowing God's dream involves a prophetic mindset. We must lean into the Father with eyes wide open to see what He would say to us. We must pursue His vision, His voice, His mind, and His heart for people.

One of the most vital dimensions of the prophetic is the realm of sight. We are spirit beings. The very DNA of God is on the inside of us. This miracle happened during the new birth. God took our dead human spirits and, in a moment of time, by faith in the resurrection of Jesus Christ and in His power, we were re-created. We were reborn in the image, in the likeness, of God, and we now carry the legacy of the Creator of the universe.

> ...that, in reference to your former manner of life, you lay aside the old self, which is being corrupted in accordance with the lusts of deceit, and that you be renewed in the spirit of your mind, and put on the new self, which in the likeness of God has been created in righteousness and holiness of the truth.
> —Ephesians 4:22–24

This laying aside of the old self and the putting on of the new is part of our rebirth, but the renewing of our minds is critical because it allows us access to the mind of God and His point of view.

> And do not be conformed to this world, but be transformed by the renewing of your mind, so that you may prove what the will of God is, that which is good and acceptable and perfect.
>
> —Romans 12:2

PERSPECTIVE

One of the challenges of living in a prophetic reality is the limitation of the human perspective. Simply put, it is impossible to fully experience and live out the destiny of God for your life while living trapped in the confines of human understanding. The prophetic will push you far beyond the limitations of your carnal thinking and vantage point. It will demand that you rise higher into another level of sight.

Your perspective must change as you stop living in the realm of the carnal and start learning to stand in the dimension of the Spirit. One definition of the word *perspective* is "the appearance to the eye of objects in respect to their relative distance and positions."[1] God's dream is expressed through a vision in revelation. To properly process divine communication, we must learn to see through the eyes of the Spirit. We simply cannot afford to pollute a prophetic perspective with limited vision or an unrenewed mind.

When a Pharisee named Nicodemus came to see Him, Jesus told him something that appeared both radical and impossible:

> Unless one is born again he cannot see the kingdom of God.
>
> —John 3:3

Nicodemus understandably questioned how being born again was even possible. Jesus responded:

> Truly, truly, I say to you, unless one is born of water and the Spirit he cannot enter into the kingdom of God. That which is born of the flesh is flesh, and that which is born of the Spirit is spirit. Do not be amazed that I said to you, "You must be born again." The wind blows where it wishes and you hear the sound of it, but do not know where it comes from and where it is going; so is everyone who is born of the Spirit.
>
> —John 3:5–8

In these statements Jesus was revealing a rich understanding of the born-again experience. He was stating that the entry point into the kingdom of God is salvation. The problem for many in modern Christianity is they simply do not understand the complexity of salvation and the totality of the redemption that takes place. Far too many estimate salvation as a get-out-of-jail-free card. They quickly run to Jesus to escape the flames of hell. While that is perhaps one of the most extravagant benefits of being born again, salvation encompasses a brand new way of life.

We are to be born of the Spirit. During the born-again experience, our inner man is changed in the twinkling of an eye. We are caught up in the Lord, no longer bound by sin and bondage. Our very nature is totally transformed. In fact, much of the time when we are combatting sin and temptation, we are missing the victory that's already been provided for us. If we learned how to live out of our new natures, we would soar above the current battles in our lives. The truth is we are no longer sitting in the old carnal way of thinking and living. We are now seated in Christ Jesus in heavenly places, ruling and reigning with Him.

> But God, being rich in mercy, because of His great love with which He loved us…raised us up with Him, and seated us with Him in the heavenly places in Christ Jesus.
> —Ephesians 2: 4, 6

There has been a change of position; therefore, there must be a change of perspective. The things of the Spirit simply cannot be comprehended by an unrenewed mind. Our minds must be washed with the water of the Word of God so that we have proper understanding of the ways of God.

> Christ also loved the church and gave Himself up for her, so that He might sanctify her, having cleansed her by the washing of water with the word.
> —Ephesians 5:25–26

We must have a rich spirit life that includes worship, the Word, and prayer. We must spend quality time praying in the Holy Ghost. When we fellowship with the third part of the Godhead, we saturate ourselves in revelation and impartation. As we pray in the Spirit, we are lifted far above the bounds of earth. We are lifted into heavenly places in our thinking, in our living, and in our spiritual lives.

Prophetic people are spirit people! They do not dwell in the earth realm exclusively. They live, move, and breathe in Christ Jesus. They have a different perspective. They see beyond the natural realm as the veil of the flesh has been torn and their spirits activated. To be truly prophetic means that you have escaped the limited sight of this earthly realm and have chosen to partner with the source of all revelation and inspiration—God Himself! There has been an exchange of perspectives. You have exchanged your limited understanding, thinking, and sight for His unlimited revelation, understanding, and vision. This type of thought process confounds the natural mind but is comprehended by the mind of the Spirit, which you have freely received through the born-again experience.

The prophetic is much more than just a simple ministry. It's a way of life and a state of being. It is the ability to see beyond what stands in front of us in the natural realm and see what appears deep in unknown mysteries and hidden agendas. It is the divine capability to see the reality of the unseen realm and to partner with heaven's plans and purposes on earth. I believe it is the desire of the Father to empower His people, the church, to live out of their new natures. He longs to enable us to come into the reality of who we are and whose we are. Part of this journey requires becoming intentional about engaging the realm of prophetic sight. We must understand that we were born to see what we need to see in order to accomplish all that God has set in front of us.

As children of God, we are carriers of His power and authority. This is how we partner with heaven in exploits—by understanding that the DNA of our Father belongs to us. We have been endued with power and entrusted with divine ability.

Jesus is seated at the right hand of the Father. He triumphed over the hierarchy of hell and stripped the enemy of his authority. We can rule and reign through Christ. Simply put, we do not fight *for* victory, but we fight *from* victory. Now the obvious question is, Why do we fight at all? The answer is simple: the enemy still has operations in the earth realm. He comes in as he is permitted through legal rights. This is why we must understand the ways of the Lord and slam the doors shut.

Jesus is the head of the church, and we are His body in the earth. We are to take territories and dream with God. We are to move in the timing and rhythm of the Lord. We are to tune into His heart and pursue His leading with all of our might. This means surrender to God and to His plans, individually and corporately. Submitting to the will of God and coming into alignment with His mandate are critical steps to reclaim the ground.

Rebellion is the act of going against God.

> An evil man seeks only rebellion; therefore a cruel messenger will be sent against him.
> —Proverbs 17:11, NKJV

Unfortunately rebellion is a typical mindset in today's society. It is one of the most challenging areas of Christianity for people who have been raised in a secular world. We are inundated with messages about doing what feels right to us. We continually hear people sharing "their truth." This mindset eradicates the fundamental understanding of absolute truth. It creates a world in which each individual does what he or she feels is best. While this may sound good and appeal to our flesh, it goes entirely against the will of God. Rebellion is the dead center of witchcraft.

> For rebellion is as the sin of witchcraft.
> —1 Samuel 15:23, NKJV

The very act of witchcraft is an act of defiance against God. While it is easy to recognize overt witchcraft, there are other more subversive forms of covert witchcraft. Many believers don't realize when they are operating in manipulation, control, and rebellion. They cling to messages about love and acceptance but shun messages of repentance and purity. This is a deceptive trap, designed to take them out of the will of God.

THE IMPORTANCE OF ALIGNMENT

One of the challenges of regional transformation is lack of

alignment. The Bible reveals a clear order for the ministries and operations of the church.

> And God has appointed in the church, first apostles, second prophets, third teachers, then miracles, then gifts of healings, helps, administrations, various kinds of tongues.
> —1 Corinthians 12:28

A thorough understanding of the apostolic ministry reveals that apostles operate in God's order and establish the church of the Lord through the declaration of the written Word of God and revelation of the voice of God speaking in the earth today. Prophetic ministry, at its pinnacle, also establishes His divine order by conveying the mind and thoughts of God.

Many times, when there is a demonic habitation in a territory or even the life of a person, the person or people group has come out of alignment with God's plan. As the apostolic anointing begins to set things in order, it can feel like a spiritual chiropractic adjustment. Though painful for the moment, it has long-lasting results that bring health and vitality to the *ekklesia*, the assembly of believers. Many believers with a shallow root system will run from this concept.

When we claim the ground, demonic access points must be closed. The role of pure prophetic ministry in this endeavor cannot be overestimated. The sight and voices of the prophets can help reveal breaches in the corporate church in a region. In the same way, a valid prophetic ministry can reveal things in our individual hearts that have created open doorways to the powers of hell. Deliverance means closing those doorways and restoring the walls of the Word of God to develop a stronghold of faith in our lives, individually and corporately.

Proverbs declares that there is a level of human thinking that seems right unto man but ultimately leads to spiritual death.

> There is a way that seems right to a man, but its end is the way of death.
>
> —Proverbs 14:12, NKJV

Letting go of carnal thinking is one of the great acts of deliverance that needs to take place to reclaim ground properly. Men and women must surrender to the Lord in their thought processes and belief systems. God challenges us to let go of systems of thought associated with demonic strongholds. Many times in the work of corporate transformation, there will be teaching that confronts religious ideologies, humanistic thinking, and ungodly belief systems. As the truth forcefully meets the presence of a lie, the power of hell will attempt to shut down the operation of truth, for revelation holds power to unlock life-changing transformation. The enemy fights not just the revelation but the measure of redemption released in the life of a person or a corporate body. The apostolic ministry seeks to bring alignment, surrender, and repentance to close down open doorways that have invited in the power of the enemy. Throughout this process there will be manifestations of spiritual warfare. It's essential to recognize the battle is not against flesh and blood but demonic entities.

> For we do not wrestle against flesh and blood, but against principalities, against powers, against the rulers of the darkness of this age, against spiritual hosts of wickedness in the heavenly places.
> —Ephesians 6:12, NKJV

The work of alignment requires patience, prayer, and perseverance. The process of yielding and surrender leads believers to a place where the Holy Spirit can work even more in their lives. As a group of people begins to navigate the process of surrender and alignment, the presence of God will surround them, eradicating the lies of the enemy. As God leads His people to a place of surrender, it can feel painful at the moment, but it's absolutely necessary for lasting results.

TUNE IN

In the Book of Revelation Jesus addressed seven churches, speaking to churches in seven particular cities, beginning with the church of Ephesus. These were prophetic edicts delivered to these regions. The head of the church was speaking to His people.

> To the angel of the church of Ephesus write, "These things says He who holds the seven stars in His right hand, who walks in the midst of the seven golden lampstands.…He who has an ear, let him hear what the Spirit says to the churches. To him who overcomes I will give to eat from the tree of life, which is in the midst of the Paradise of God."
> —Revelation 2:1, 7, NKJV

Jesus instructed those who have an ear to hear to listen closely. It is an invitation to revelation and to opening up another dimension in regions. For far too long we have prayed for people and situations—both of which are important—but we have stayed at ground level. There is another dimension of something profound in the prophetic ministry for groups and places.

We need ears and eyes that are tuned in and purposefully peering into the dimension of the spirit. We need to become adept at capturing God's mind and heart for a people and a place. Prophetic words are hovering over each place, just waiting for an activated bride to come up higher and hear what the Lord would say.

When I travel on assignment, I often ask the Father, "What are You saying to this territory?" Most of the time, it is a matter of my rediscovering what He has already said. As I quiet my mind and become aware of the presence of God, I suddenly hear or see something profound. These revelations are like small spiritual keys that must be taken and put in the doorway to step fully into the revelation for a people and a locale.

Chapter 3

DIVINE PARTNERS

I find it particularly helpful when there is a prophet laboring with me. The ox and the eagle together access might and sight. There is an awareness of the prophetic purpose of God along with apostolic wisdom and strategy to labor in agreement with the Word. When there is apostolic might without prophetic revelation, there is an abundance of labor filled with friction because there is a deficiency of oil. When there is a high level of prophetic revelation without a vivid apostolic blueprint, you end up with an unstable people who see and know but are unable to produce what they know. It is the full cooperation and partnership of the apostolic and prophetic, along with the other ministry gifts and the activation of the believers, that creates an unstoppable kingdom structure.

The apostolic is a ministry and mantle. It is critical that those carrying it receive clear direction on the where and the how. This is where the prophetic comes in. We need leaders in this day who will pay attention to their dreams and night visions—leaders such as Joseph, who dreamed a dream, and the Apostle Paul, who had a night vision concerning Macedonia. I am convinced that the ministry of dreams and visions are apostolic battle weapons that clarify assignments and purposes for territories. We need prophets who will boldly speak forth what the Lord reveals to them. When there is clear prophetic direction and insight, the momentum is unstoppable. Prophetic ministry is an invaluable asset to emerging apostles as well as established apostles. Far too often the enemy is successful at dividing apostles and prophets because of their different perspectives in the kingdom.

DIFFERENT ROLES, SAME GOAL

The apostolic anointing is primarily a building and governing anointing. Apostles serve as God's generals, boldly forging a new way forward. They are not intimidated by demonic strongholds and rulers. Their decree is decisive, and their preaching is confrontational. They are strategic, vision-driven builders. They have no time or place for complacency. The apostolic mandate is one of rapid-fire advancement in supernatural building. Apostolic ministries refuse stagnation and continue to grow with a strong mandate of reform. This mindset often challenges those who come in their midst and are not used to a strong apostolic anointing. Due to the visionary nature of apostles, they can often move in a hurried fashion. This is part of their divine makeup. Once they have heard from heaven, they are convinced of God's direction. They unashamedly step out in faith in order to advance the kingdom of God.

On the other hand, prophets live in the realm of revelation and intimacy. They have no time or place for religious political mindsets. Their primary aim is to be close to the Lord and hear from Him. Depending on their unique prophetic makeup, they often have a variety of deeply spiritual encounters with the Lord. Authentic prophets long to call the bride back to the Bridegroom. Their message is one of intimacy and passion for His presence.

> O God, You are my God; I shall seek You earnestly; my soul thirsts for You, my flesh yearns for You, in a dry and weary land where there is

> no water. Thus I have seen You in the sanctuary, to see Your power and Your glory. Because Your lovingkindness is better than life, my lips will praise You. So I will bless You as long as I live; I will lift up my hands in Your name. My soul is satisfied as with marrow and fatness, and my mouth offers praises with joyful lips. When I remember You on my bed, I meditate on You in the night watches, for You have been my help, and in the shadow of Your wings I sing for joy. My soul clings to You; Your right hand upholds me.
>
> —Psalm 63:1–8

This psalm of David reveals his utter dependence on the presence of God for survival and satisfaction. To properly understand the depth of David's relationship with God, one would have to do a survey of his life. The presence of God was the very thing that sustained David in the greatest times of adversity.

> You will make known to me the path of life; in Your presence is fullness of joy; in Your right hand there are pleasures forever.
>
> —Psalm 16:11

> Even though I walk through the valley of the shadow of death, I fear no evil, for You are with me; Your rod and Your staff, they comfort me.
> —Psalm 23:4

> Where can I go from Your Spirit? Or where can I flee from Your presence? If I ascend to heaven, You are there; if I make my bed in Sheol, behold, You are there. If I take the wings of the dawn, if I dwell in the remotest part of the sea, even there Your hand will lead me, and Your right hand will lay hold of me.
> —Psalm 139:7–10

David was an authentic worshipper who lived to dwell in the glory of God. David carried a prophetic anointing upon his life as a psalmist. His writings urge the reader to press deeper into the things of God. This is a common trait of prophets. They enjoy the presence of God and esteem it above all other things. Their message is one that draws people back to their first love, Jesus. The mantle of the prophet is highly revelatory and carries with it an extreme passion for God and God alone. This is why the role of prophets in apostolic work is so critical.

It is easy for an apostolic work to become dry and burdened primarily with the vision of building objectives. The apostle as a master strategist and planner continually dreams of exploits to reclaim ground from the grip of darkness. Apostles are bold in their approach and typically have a strong measure of faith. They urge their spiritual family to launch deeper into the realm of raw faith and believe God for outrageous things. In the midst of all the work and labor, God uses the voice of prophets to call the people back to the place of intimacy, to His presence.

The unique relationship between apostles and prophets is a vital component of kingdom work. When apostles and prophets work together, they are absolutely unstoppable and a tremendous threat to the kingdom of darkness. But they can end up becoming divided because of their perspectives. For example, oftentimes apostles will grow frustrated with prophets due to their lack of momentum. The apostle can feel as though the prophet is moving too slowly and is caught up in the clouds instead of strategizing for wise kingdom building. Conversely the prophet can easily be frustrated with the apostle, often as a result of the apostolic building tenacity. Prophets can feel as though apostles are moving too quickly and don't have a strong enough value system for intimacy and the Word of the Lord. Along with these spiritual perspectives, tension can also arise due to natural personality conflicts. It is imperative that there is a set man or woman on an apostolic team who has the final say. While each team member is valuable and holds a unique place on the team, there should be a senior leader who has the authority to make the final decisions. In a healthy way that apostolic leader should lean on the prophet for perspective and insight to implement wise building plans. The alignment of apostles and prophets strengthens the function of prophets and enhances their ability to build the kingdom of God. The key to long-term success in a relationship between apostles and prophets is mutual respect and value for others' unique differences and perspectives. In addition, a strong personal relationship is a critical component for healthy alignment.

A mature apostolic-prophetic partnership creates a solid foundation. As these two foundational gifts partner together for kingdom advancement, they also activate, appoint, and release the other fivefold ministry gifts. When the fivefold ministry and kingdom-minded believers unite to fulfill a common objective, there is a true apostolic company with the potential to bring massive reformation to a territory or sphere of influence. This is the objective in this hour.

Chapter 4

RECLAIMING GEOGRAPHICAL TERRITORIES

Let's dive in deeper to the concept of reclaiming the ground in a geographical territory. You cannot properly understand apostolic ministry without recognizing the sending mandate. At its most foundational level, apostolic ministry revolves around the concept of being sent and sending. Apostles and apostolic leaders are often sent to unique geographical territories with the mandate of transformation. But there is a level of warfare that occurs when an apostolic company contends for a region.

This type of fight is not for the faint at heart. It is time consuming and laborious. It demands continual prayer and the refreshing that only comes in the presence of the Lord. Strategy for regional transformation is imperative in this work. Strong and vibrant worship is critical to bring the presence of the Lord and much-needed refreshing. Sound prophetic words and insight are key components to unlock God's plan for regions and territories. Now, let's establish two key foundations that must be understood in order to embrace the concept of reclaiming physical ground.

Number one, we must acknowledge the reality that demonic entities inhabit both individuals and territories, manifesting their wicked desires and evil influences. There are large segments of the church that simply do not believe in this concept. Yet when we look at the ministry of Jesus, we see deliverance as one of the continual flows. Far too many today discount the ministry of deliverance and the reality of demonic beings. It is impossible to advance the kingdom of God without conflict with evil spirits. I believe the Lord is raising up a fierce and bold church that is not afraid to confront the powers of hell. This is what I call ground-level warfare. It is finding the devil piece by piece, person by person, and operation by operation in order to bring freedom and refreshing.

Number two, we must have a biblical understanding of principalities that attempt to rule over regions in order to establish and maintain demonic strongholds. In the case of territories, the demonic ruler has been invited in through evil covenants, past sins, and open doors that create a legal right for that demonic ruler to have a place of dominion in the territory. Now, in order to reclaim ground, these demons must be identified. This is one of the most critical functions of prophets in a regional work. They can adequately discern and see hidden demons and unholy thrones. Once these demonic rulers have been exposed and identified, the corporate work of regional deliverance begins. This is a multipronged operation of spiritual warfare that involves changing the spiritual climate and mobilizing the ekklesia via territorial- or strategic-level warfare.

Jesus warned His followers about Satan's position in this world.

> Now judgment is upon this world; now the ruler of this world will be cast out.
> —John 12:31

> I will not speak much more with you, for the ruler of the world is coming, and he has nothing in Me.
> —John 14:30

In both of these passages Jesus established the reality that Satan was given a place of rule in this earthly world. This position of authority was granted to him through the transgression of Adam and Eve in the garden. Before that, Satan had no authority in the earth because God had given dominion to Adam and Eve, His choice creations. It was the plan of the enemy to entice Adam and Eve into partnering with his evil desires, and they unfortunately fell into his trap. However, as a result of the fall, Jesus came as the second Adam to defeat the powers of hell and return man to the position of dominion that God ordained. And out of that dominion comes the ministry of deliverance, in which we enforce kingdom authority and drive the devil out. During the process of identification and ultimately expulsion, there must be a breaking of all legal ties that have permitted the devil to exist in a space or territory.

Satan is the god of this world. The Apostle Paul revealed Satan's evil operations to the church at Corinth, stating that the enemy has blinded the eyes of people to the light of the gospel of Christ.

> ...in whose case the god of this world has blinded the minds of the unbelieving so that they might not see the light of the gospel of the glory of Christ, who is the image of God.
> —2 Corinthians 4:4

The intention of the enemy in regions and territories is to blind eyes to foundational truth. The enemy also attempts to create a stronghold—a system of thoughts, philosophies, and ways of thinking in the human mind. Demonized people in a region will often stay stuck in a cycle of recurring failure because they are trapped in ungodly thought processes. This is why one of the most potent tools in reformation is the ministry of the teacher to lay a solid foundation of the truth of the Word of God. As the teacher ministers, the truth and light of God's Word shines forth, displacing the power of hell. This is true not only in the lives of individuals as we engage in ground-level warfare but also in regional warfare.

PREACHING AND TEACHING

God raises up both strong preaching and strong teaching of His Word in a territory. The two ministries have two different intents. Preaching is the declaration of spiritual truth accompanied by supernatural power. A preacher under the anointing of the Holy Spirit declares, challenges, and confronts. There is a deliverance element present in the operation of true preaching. Teaching is entirely different as it unveils the mind of God through more in-depth understanding of the written Word of God. The teacher lays out foundations and truths that wash deception out of the mind of the believer. A seasoned apostle will always recognize the validity of teaching and establish at least one person on his or her team with the fivefold ministry gift of teaching so that people can come out from under the operation of the regional stronghold.

To effectively reclaim geographical territories, we must understand the structural operations of the kingdom of darkness.

> For we wrestle not against flesh and blood, but against principalities, against powers, against the rulers of the darkness of this world, against spiritual wickedness in high places.
> —Ephesians 6:12, KJV

All too often believers have a wrong concept of the enemy's camp. They think of demons as unorganized, roaming beings when in fact there is a hierarchy to the forces of hell. Satan has militarized and organized his troops, with principalities in control of leagues of demons to influence and impact territories.

It's also vital to understand that the kingdom of darkness is comprised of many demonic entities. I do not say this to instigate fear, because the true reality is found in the kingdom of light, and the power of our God triumphs over the kingdom of darkness every single time. The complete work of Jesus gave the people of God legislative authority over the kingdom of darkness. We never fight from a place of defeat, but we move forward in boldness, enforcing the legislative authority of our God. We study spiritual warfare not to exalt the kingdom of darkness but to have a better theological grounding in God's combat rules so that we can enjoy the fullness of His promise in our lives individually and corporately.

Jesus demonstrated the authority we have as believers during His encounter with the man we know as the demoniac of the Gadarenes.

> When He got out of the boat, immediately a man from the tombs with an unclean spirit met Him, and he had his dwelling among the tombs. And no one was able to bind him anymore, even with a chain.... Constantly, night and day, he was screaming among the tombs and in the mountains, and gashing himself with stones. Seeing Jesus from a distance, he ran up and bowed down before Him; and shouting with a loud voice, he said, "What business do we have with each other, Jesus, Son of the Most High God? I implore You by God, do not torment

me!" For He had been saying to him, "Come out of the man, you unclean spirit!" And He was asking him, "What is your name?" And he said to Him, "My name is Legion; for we are many." And he began to implore Him earnestly not to send them out of the country. Now there was a large herd of swine feeding nearby on the mountain. The demons implored Him, saying, "Send us into the swine so that we may enter them." Jesus gave them permission. And coming out, the unclean spirits entered the swine; and the herd rushed down the steep bank into the sea, about two thousand of them; and they were drowned in the sea.

—Mark 5:2–13

There is a significant piece of truth captured in this particular verse as Jesus spoke to the ruling demon inside of the man. The demon revealed that it was not alone, but there was in fact a legion of demons inhabiting this one individual. Further inspection of the word *legion* reveals that it could be over six thousand demons.[2] Imagine that many demons in one person. If six thousand demons could be inside of one man, then it would stand to reason that there are potentially millions of dark spirits of various kinds. Again, this is not to bring fear but clarity as we understand that there are a variety of demons in operation that ultimately impact and influence individuals, societies, regions, and nations. Our assignment is to boldly believe Jesus Christ and exercise the authority that He has given to us with wisdom and precision to bring reformation and kingdom advancement, both on individual and corporate levels.

Spiritual warfare is the result of activated believers going forth, unafraid of the enemy and mantled with the power of the risen Christ. The corporate church should make a difference in the territory it occupies, and the apostolic anointing is one of the keys to making that difference. The apostolic anointing is one of transformation and change. Apostolic churches are not content to just fill a building and leave the region unchanged. They preach, teach, and equip believers to be fully activated and to corporately push back the powers of darkness with a vision to displace the ruling spirits and release the kingdom of God in a fresh and new way in the territory.

THE MANDATE

There are several vital components in territorial transformation. It begins with God-ordained vision and conviction. Without apostolic clarity of the mission at hand, people will wander in a seemingly unending wilderness of confusion. This is why God assigns a bold apostolic leader with a call from heaven to a region. This leader does not come to cater to popular opinion or take a survey of the people in the region but instead comes with a mandate from God. Every apostle will move only by mandate. One of my favorite Old Testament examples of a God-given mandate is found in the Book of Nehemiah. When Nehemiah heard about the state of Jerusalem—with the people in distress, the walls broken down, and the gates burned—he wept and mourned, fasted and prayed.

> I pray, LORD God of heaven, O great and awesome God, You who keep Your covenant and mercy with those who love You and observe Your commandments....Remember, I pray, the word that You commanded Your servant Moses, saying, "If you...return to Me, and keep My commandments and do them, though some of you were cast out to the farthest part of the heavens, yet I will gather them from there, and bring them to the place which I have chosen as a dwelling for My name."
> —Nehemiah 1:5, 8–9, NKJV

In a time of destruction Nehemiah received a mandate and a burden to rebuild. People thought he was crazy and confused, but he was far from it. He was focused on his God-ordained purpose. He was bold and unwavering because of the clear call he received from the Lord. We need bold apostolic leaders in this generation who will receive clear calls from God and be unwavering in their convictions.

> And I said to the king, "If it pleases the king, and if your servant has found favor in your sight, I ask that you send me to Judah, to the city of my fathers' tombs, that I may rebuild it."
>
> Then the king said to me (the queen also sitting beside him), "How long will your journey be? And when will you return?" So it pleased the king to send me; and I set him a time.
>
> —Nehemiah 2:5–6, NKJV

Nehemiah, as an Old Testament type of an apostle, was driven by the mandate he had received from heaven. This is a common trait of apostolic leaders. They are uncommon in their pursuit of the mandates they have received from God, and they will issue bold calls to the people to build and advance the kingdom of God in a place or space. Apostolic leaders infuse people in their apostolic company with vision. Apostles are visionaries who understand that provision is commanded by vision. After all, faith is a creative force. By faith we believe God and move forward, undeterred by opposition or a seeming lack of resources. It is with the spirit of faith that we speak to storms and mountains. It is with the spirit of faith that we command resources to fulfill the vision to come forth. It is by faith that our eyes can see beyond the current limitations and see the vision fulfilled.

The apostolic anointing is a strong anointing that can withstand persecution and attacks. One of the attributes of the apostolic is the tenacity for the mandate of God. Strong apostles will infuse the people they are leading with apostolic stamina. Simply put, this is the ox anointing. It is the ability to plow the dry and hard ground.

> For it is written in the law of Moses, "You shall not muzzle an ox while it treads out the grain." Is it oxen God is concerned about?
> —1 Corinthians 9:9, NKJV

In this passage, the Apostle Paul is writing about apostolic ministry, and he uses the prophetic picture of the ox as an example. I believe this is because he's painting a vivid word picture. The ox is a laboring animal known for its strength and ability to endure. These are apostolic cornerstones. In the work of regional transformation, patience is a key ingredient along with strength. As we've already discussed, regional change will include regional warfare as the principality begins to oppose the work that is happening. This is evident in the story of Nehemiah because the enemies of the work started to show up to mock, accuse, and attack.

> But when Sanballat the Horonite and Tobiah the Ammonite official, and Geshem the Arab heard it, they mocked us and despised us.
> —Nehemiah 2:19

> Now it came about that when Sanballat heard that we were rebuilding the wall, he became furious and very angry and mocked the Jews. He spoke in the presence of his brothers and the wealthy men of Samaria and said, "What are these feeble Jews doing? Are they going to restore it for themselves? Can they offer sacrifices? Can they finish in a day? Can they

> revive the stones from the dusty rubble even the burned ones?" Now Tobiah the Ammonite was near him and he said, "Even what they are building—if a fox should jump on it, he would break their stone wall down!"
>
> —Nehemiah 4:1–3

Warfare is often an indicator of the ruling spirit or spirits over a territory. All too often apostolic companies shrink under the weight of the warfare. It's understandable, but we must develop a more robust spiritual warfare grid. Spiritual warfare in a new territory can reveal the operations of demonic entities that were previously hidden. The transformation leader must identify what the ruling enemy is in the territory. When I step into particular anointings or modes of operation, what is the level of resistance?

I remember when I planted my first church in a religious territory, and the warfare was fierce. As I observed specific trends, I was able to accurately identify the enemy I was up against. It seemed as though every time I engaged a more profound prophetic anointing, there was a harsh and swift retaliatory attack. The attack was also ferocious as I labored apostolically to raise a fivefold ministry center with an apostle at the helm. It was evident to me that we were dealing with a religious spirit. The region was firmly rooted in ungodly traditions and evil mindsets. I was able to take a spiritual inventory of the enemy's ploys against me and the work I was building to bring exposure to the particular demonic influences of the region.

One thing you must realize in the work of taking back the ground in a region is that oftentimes the opinions of people in the territory have been influenced by the stronghold or system of thoughts connected to the ruling spirit. Therefore, people in local church communities will place pressure on the apostolic leader to do church in the way they are familiar with. This is often a mindset that has been developed by the ruling spirit in the territory. As a leader trying to build a kingdom work and gain a faithful following, it is tempting to submit to the opinions of the people. On a human level everybody wants acceptance, yet this could form a toxic alliance with an evil ruler.

I remember laboring in that religious territory and people telling me to stop prophesying; they just wanted me to teach. They did not receive the office of an apostle or a prophet, but they loved the office of a teacher. Even though they did not recognize a demonic entity was influencing their opinions, I did. So I had to stand and resist the temptation to cater to the will of the people. In building a robust apostolic hub, there must be love and compassion for the people of God, but there must be a commitment to the mandate of the head of the church, the Lord Jesus Christ. We must be continuously reminded that He sent us, He mandated us, and He will protect us. There is no room for wavering or being deterred from the appointed pathway the Lord Jesus has set before us.

Chapter 5

TEARING DOWN EVIL ALTARS

When the Lord brought Israel out of Egypt and to the Promised Land, He instructed Israel to tear down the demonic altars and to utterly destroy every place in the nation where legal entry was given to demonic rulers.

> Ye shall utterly destroy all the places, wherein the nations which ye shall possess served their gods, upon the high mountains, and upon the hills, and under every green tree: and ye shall overthrow their altars, and break their pillars,

> and burn their groves with fire; and ye shall hew down the graven images of their gods, and destroy the names of them out of that place.
> —Deuteronomy 12:2–3, KJV

These verses shed much-needed light on open doors that are established through idolatry, wickedness, and iniquity in a region. The Lord was telling His people to rid the land of any unclean altars, graven images, or points of contact for idol worship of demonic entities. In deliverance ministry, legal doors must be closed. Often, when regional deliverance is occurring, the Spirit of God will begin to show people where doorways have been opened—and prayers of repentance and cleansing are necessary to close those doors. There are times the Lord will assign apostolic intercessors to go out to physical places to redeem the land and release the power of the blood of Jesus. Many believers who do not understand these practices will think the intercessors have lost their minds, but intercession is a biblical practice. Do you remember Nehemiah's prayer when he found out about the state of Jerusalem? He interceded on behalf of the land and his people (Neh. 1:4–11). And then there was Daniel. He had been taken captive and carried off to Babylon, yet he was moved to intercede to the Lord on behalf of his people and their land.

> Alas, O Lord, the great and awesome God, who keeps His covenant and lovingkindness for those who love Him and keep His commandments, we have sinned, committed iniquity, acted wickedly and rebelled, even turning aside from Your commandments and ordinances. Moreover, we have not listened to Your servants the prophets, who spoke in Your name to our kings, our princes, our fathers and all the people of the land.…O my God, incline Your ear and hear! Open Your eyes and see our desolations and the city which is called by Your name; for we are not presenting our supplications before You on account of any merits of our own, but on account of Your great compassion. O Lord, hear! O Lord, forgive! O Lord, listen and take action! For Your own sake, O my God, do not delay, because Your city and Your people are called by Your name.
> —Daniel 9:4–6, 18–19

God calls His people out of idol worship to come back to a place of purity with Him.

And Samuel spake unto all the house of Israel, saying, If ye do return unto the LORD with all your hearts, then put away the strange gods and Ashtaroth from among you, and prepare your hearts unto the LORD, and serve him only: and he will deliver you out of the hand of the Philistines. Then the children of Israel did put away Baalim and Ashtaroth, and served the LORD only.
—1 Samuel 7:3–4, KJV

Therefore, my beloved, flee from idolatry.
—1 Corinthians 10:14

The Word of God tells us that our God is a jealous God.

You shall not worship any other god, for the LORD, whose name is Jealous, is a jealous God.
—Exodus 34:14

This doesn't mean that God is jealous over us but rather jealous for us. He wants our full affection and attention. Throughout the Word of God, we are admonished again and again to turn away from all other gods and serve the one true living God.

There is no room for idolatry in the life of a believer. Many times, as we're reclaiming pieces of the ground, the Lord will allow us to see previous acts of idolatry or areas where the church has knowingly or unknowingly partnered with ruling spirits in the territory. He will call His people out of that. Acts of repentance or turning away are often necessary.

> "Yet you have forsaken Me and served other gods; therefore I will no longer deliver you. Go and cry out to the gods which you have chosen; let them deliver you in the time of your distress." The sons of Israel said to the LORD, "We have sinned, do to us whatever seems good to You; only please deliver us this day." So they put away the foreign gods from among them and served the LORD; and He could bear the misery of Israel no longer.
> —Judges 10:13–16

During the time of the judges, the Lord once again had to deal with a backslidden Israel. They had turned to other gods. They had abandoned their covenant with God due to their lust. This is often the case with the roots of idolatry. Man, left to himself without the nature of God working in and through him, will yield to carnal desires and temptations. The Lord was angry with Israel because, despite His mighty hand of deliverance in their midst, they still turned to other gods.

IDOLATRY

One of the ways demon rulers are empowered in territories is through the people's participation in idolatry. The idolatry can occur on a variety of fronts. It has often been initiated by previous generations and willing acts of placing other gods before the Lord. In some regions it may be the willing participation of city leaders in the occult. In other regions it may be the heavy influence of perversion that traces back generations and is currently the standard in the territory. This is why educated intercessors and prophets are essential; they have to be able to both discern and study the history of the land, along with having a present-day understanding of the promises of God for the region.

When prophetic people move into a particular territory, they often will begin to experience mental and emotional warfare based on the thrones and dominions that have been established in the region. I do not say this to empower or glorify the camp of the enemy in any way. Let me be clear and state this boldly: Jesus paid the total price for your absolute victory in redemption. No matter how demonized a region or territory is, as a believer you have the right to soar above it all. You can live out of your new nature and partner with the promises of the written Word of God to conquer the effects of strongholds in your region. Having said this, I also think it's important to properly discern the warfare happening in the mind based upon the thrones and dominions in a region.

I remember being in a particular region that from the outside appeared to be a very godly area. There was an abundance of churches and a lot of professing Christians. Yet the power of God was in short supply in the territory. Prophets and prophetic ministry were widely rejected. Spirit-filled living was shunned and replaced with complacent Christianity. Passionate churches were not welcomed. The dominant type of church in the region was one with watered-down preaching and worship to accommodate a lukewarm atmosphere.

Further inspection of the region revealed that there were a lot of old occult practices mixed in with the church. There were also strongholds of religion, racism, and tradition. There were thrones built to these idols. You could preach and teach without identifying these strongholds, and the warfare would be minimal, but when you identified these demonic strongholds, the retaliatory warfare was immense.

Demon rulers establish systems of thought to bind the minds of the people of God. The enemy understands the power of thoughts and belief systems. Each territory has its unique stronghold in the lives of believers that must be dismantled by proper teaching and by renewing the mind. This must be understood by those endeavoring to reclaim the ground and territory. The ground is not just the soil under your feet but also the hearts of men, the center of thought and reason, the imagination, and the creative potential of the mind. There must be a focus on deliverance in the area of thinking. Breakthrough churches and hubs must preach and teach strong messages of redemption and victory to liberate the people of God. They must systematically and methodically go against the grain in the region.

As Elijah was squaring off against the false prophets on Mount Carmel, he called for the prophets of the groves.

> Now therefore send, and gather to me all Israel unto mount Carmel, and the prophets of Baal four hundred and fifty, and the prophets of the groves four hundred, which eat at Jezebel's table.
> —1 Kings 18:19, KJV

The groves were places of idol worship where the images of a wooden female goddess were worshipped. Entangled in this idolatry were spirits of seduction representing sensuality and sexuality. The prophets of the groves were unclean because they were involved in establishing evil altars in the territory. They openly worshipped false gods in the wilderness. They aimed to marry the land, or the geographical territory, to demons of sexuality. These spirits inhabited the vile altars established through false prophetic ministry. It was a pure prophet who dared to confront what others were overlooking. As I have always said, prophets are true spiritual warriors. They see the demons hiding in the corner.

The work of reclaiming ground is arduous. It is not for the faint at heart. When there has been an abundance of idol worship and false gods along with impure thinking, there is an evil covenant established in the region. Simply put, the land has been married to false gods. Part of the redemption process is uncovering the evil acts, establishing an altar to the living God, and cleansing the region through prayer, intercession, and worship. One of the things the ekklesia can do in a region is to marry the land to the Lord, the one true God. Through prayer the church can reestablish the covenant of the Lord God Almighty in the territory. Just as the fire from heaven fell upon the altar that Elijah built, so will the fire of God fall upon a church, a hub, or a regional apostolic base that reestablishes God's covenant in a territory.

THE POWER OF WORDS

As the covenant of the Lord is established in the geographical space, the ways of the Lord will also be established in the hearts of the people. While these acts involve spiritual legalities—meaning understanding laws that govern warfare and deliverance—one of the primary catalysts for revival and transformation must be the law of the Spirit. There must be a sound theological grasp of the grace of God and the completed work of Jesus at the cross. Authentic spiritual warfare with a balanced and healthy theological approach should feel more like an act of love than a painful task. It should look like journeying with the Father on a great adventure, not continually being exhausted or worn out. There must be a rich understanding of the goodness and grace of God. The difference between the old covenant and the new covenant is summarized in one word—*mercy*. God's mercy and rich love towards His people must be forefront in the minds of people reclaiming ground. It cannot be a work of the flesh but must be that which is born of the Spirit. And words play a powerful role in that work.

> Set a guard over my mouth, LORD; keep watch over the door of my lips.
>
> —Psalm 141:3, NIV

The power of words created everything we see in the known world. In the beginning God created with His words.

> In the beginning God created the heavens and the earth. The earth was formless and void, and darkness was over the surface of the deep, and the Spirit of God was moving over the surface of the waters. Then God said…
> —Genesis 1:1–3

His Spirit was hovering over the face of the deep. The world was in a state of chaos and confusion. What was on the heart of God? What was His intention? He was about to bring forth divine order and creativity. As we study the Word of God, we understand that everything has a time, a place, and an order. There is no confusion about the organizational structure of heaven. When we read the story of God's creation, we see that He perfectly assigned everything to its proper place and order. It is with this in mind that we understand the concept of God's order.

We also know that the ultimate aim of the enemy is to breach divine order and create confusion in the area of identity for humanity. The devil works overtime to enforce his lies in the minds of human beings and bring separation from God. How does he do it? He causes people to question their relationships with God and their role in creating with Him. He continually hurls accusations at the minds of human beings. The Bible calls him the accuser of the brethren.

> Then I heard a loud voice in heaven, saying, "Now the salvation, and the power, and the kingdom of our God and the authority of His Christ have come, for the accuser of our brethren has been thrown down, he who accuses them before our God day and night."
> —Revelation 12:10

The enemy also understands the principle of legalities. When we recognize the fact that God's kingdom operates through covenants and spiritual laws, we must then acknowledge that part of the deliverance process is the discovery of broken spiritual laws and evil covenants. One of the chief attributes of a covenant is the power of words and agreements.

It's easy to get stuck in a struggle of human activity, works, and bondage. The reality is that the old covenant law was provided to teach man that it was hopeless without Jesus Christ, that man was incapable of fulfilling the law on his own merit. The only way man could fully walk with the living God was through the grace of redemption. Adam and Eve, through their disobedience, sent humanity into a spiritual freefall. No matter how much Old Testament characters tried, they came up short—even Abraham, who chose to believe God and whose daring faith was counted as righteousness. He was a forerunner, pointing the way to Jesus Christ. Through the sacrifice of Jesus, the Lord bought back His prized creation and extended a hand of grace and mercy towards us. And because of that sacrifice, we can be born again into the kingdom by faith, which pleases God. When the gospel is preached to us and our spiritual ears hear it, faith arises in our hearts. We then speak an agreement with the promise of God, and at the sound of our voices, grace is dispatched along with the creative ability of God to provide a new nature.

The kingdom of God then comes to take up residence inside of us. We are new creations, and His authority lives in us! Because we are children of God, His power resides in us. There is no limitation to the exploits we can engage in by the power of the living God inside us.

The Lord said He would write His Word, His promises, on the tablets of our hearts. The Prophet Jeremiah foretold that when the new covenant was made, the Lord would write his Word on the hearts of His people. And the Book of Hebrews confirmed the fulfillment of that prophecy.

"Behold, days are coming," declares the LORD, "when I will make a new covenant with the house of Israel and with the house of Judah.... But this is the covenant which I will make with the house of Israel after those days," declares the LORD, "I will put My law within them and on their heart I will write it; and I will be their God, and they shall be My people."
—Jeremiah 31:31, 33

"This is the covenant that I will make with them after those days, says the Lord: I will imprint My laws upon their heart, and on their mind I will inscribe them [producing an inward change]." He then says, "And their sins and their lawless acts I will remember no more [no longer holding their sins against them]." Now where there is [absolute] forgiveness and complete cancellation of the penalty of these things, there is no longer any offering [to be made to atone] for sin.
—Hebrews 10:16–18, AMP

This is a radical departure from what occurred during the old covenant, when the Lord was unable to write His Word on the tablets of men's hearts because the sinful nature darkened them. But the new covenant changed that. With the hearts of His born-again children, God finds a canvas that can hold the ink of His lovingkindness, His mercy, and His grace. He finds hearts where He can inscribe the truth of His Word, knowing that our sins will be remembered no more because of Jesus. It is an entirely different way of living! Instead of keeping rules and regulations and relating to God as an external force, we get to walk with Him as His sons and daughters with His Spirit living inside of us. God is no longer dealing with us from the outside in but rather from the inside out. The voice of God is no longer external but internal, housed in our new nature. As we begin to understand these principles, we can fully understand the methodology of creation.

> Yet we have the same spirit of faith as he had, who wrote in Scripture, "I believed, therefore I spoke." We also believe, therefore we also speak.
> —2 Corinthians 4:13, AMP

The spirit of faith is first established in our hearts and then causes our mouths to speak. There is a connection between our minds, which are the creative centers of reasoning in our lives, and our mouths. Words are the most powerful tools given to us as children of God. They are God's chosen instruments to appropriate creative power. We believe and therefore speak! As our minds are renewed and begin to align with the will of God, our mouths should change. We should become more aware of our prophetic natures and the ability of God to work through us by speaking. But note that it is dangerous to just speak out of our emotions without prayer. This is a trap for prophetic people in particular. God touches the mouths of prophetic people, and He intends to use their words to release His kingdom on the earth. He can do this because His kingdom is abiding in the hearts of men.

Let us be aware of the creative ability that God has entrusted us with. Rather than speaking doubt and unbelief, we should speak God's promises over our lives, individually and corporately. We should take the prophetic words and promises of God for regions and people and boldly decree them. At times, we will look crazy, but we cannot be moved by what other human beings will think of us. We must stand in the conviction of the Word of God and His prophetic revelation for our lives. This is a tremendous tool in reclaiming ground in our families, in our cities, in our churches, and in our nation. The Lord invites us into a place of intercession, and we become so convinced of what He has said to us that we have the ability to stand in the midst of a storm. We become so aware of His profound promise that it fills our minds with thoughts of redemption and victory. From that place of holy conviction, we stand in opposition to the hand of the enemy and speak the will of God into the earth. Who cares if we look crazy? I'm sure Jesus looked crazy when He spoke life over Jairus's seemingly dead daughter. I'm sure the patriarchs of old looked crazy to their generations when they spoke the mysteries of God in the midst of an evil and perverted people. May we be honored to be chosen by God to stand as His beacons of light in the midst of darkness. May we be selected as creative vessels and instruments of God in the earth to speak His promise. May we have the daring type of faith that will decree what God says, no matter what our bodies feel or our minds scream. May we arise and be a people of faith!

THE POWER OF AGREEMENT

In addition to the power of words, the power of agreement is vital in tearing down evil altars and reclaiming territory for the kingdom.

> Again I say unto you, That if two of you shall agree on earth as touching any thing that they shall ask, it shall be done for them of my Father which is in heaven.
> —Matthew 18:19, KJV

> Can two walk together, except they be agreed?
>
> —Amos 3:3, KJV

Both of these Scripture verses are vivid examples of the power of agreement. In the first verse, we see that the presence of God and His divine ability rest in the midst of believers who come into agreement. This principle is established throughout the entirety of the Word of God. One of the most vivid examples is Psalm 133:

> Behold, how good and how pleasant it is for brothers to dwell together in unity! It is like the precious oil upon the head, coming down upon the beard, even Aaron's beard, coming down upon the edge of his robes. It is like the dew of Hermon coming down upon the mountains of Zion; for there the LORD commanded the blessing—life forever.

In the midst of unity, there is both a commanded blessing and a powerful flow of oil. By looking at that prophetic picture, we understand there are realms of the anointing of God for regions and people that will only come when there is agreement. In the verse from the Book of Amos, we see that two can't arrive at the same destination without an agreement. Simply put, our journey takes us to the place of finality based upon our agreement. For example, when we get born again, if we come into agreement with all that God has said about us, we are set free from the shackles and traumas of our past, and we are delivered from the work of evil. We then become unstoppable as we walk in the very promises of God and manifest the DNA of heaven that is within us. Conversely, some have been born again and heard Bible teaching, yet they continued to struggle in the most basic principles of their faith. I would present to you that one of the potential problems is what they are agreeing with.

In the ministry of deliverance, it is often necessary to identify demonic agreements in the life of an individual. For example, if a person was targeted with bullying as a child and formed an evil identity of rejection, he or she came into agreement with the false definition that the enemy placed upon his or her life. This agreement began the demonic habitation and the creation of a false identity. In most instances, people who have been bullied have decreed things out of their mouths that aligned their hearts with what the enemy said and built an emotional barrier around themselves. That barrier withholds the power of transformation, which resides in the Word of God. Once this entry point has been identified, it must be sanctified with the blood of Jesus. We can look back to the Old Testament example of placing the blood on the doorpost of every house during Passover. The doorway speaks of an entry point. We are to secure the individual entry points into our lives with the blood of Jesus, period.

Two of the most potent entry points are our ears and our eyes. We often become the product of what we give our attention, of what we continually see and hear. On a corporate level there are entry points into cities and territories that have been influenced by the voice of the adversary. People living in those territories have come into agreement with what the enemy has said, and they have become dull in the spiritual sense to what the Lord has said over their region or territory. Gatekeeper apostolic leaders are assigned to territories to close the entry points. They build strong and fortified places of truth. And prophets and prophetic decrees are crucial, as they reinvigorate the environment with the word of the Lord.

Renunciation is a necessary act in the journey of deliverance. Many times when laboring for the transformation in a region, renunciation and repentance are necessary, along with the application of the blood of Jesus to secure the gates. It is imperative that the people of God who understand their authority as believers use that authority to renounce every valid demonic agreement. Demonic vows and agreements hold the potential to keep a people and a region in bondage. Let me establish this from another angle. Remember when God called the Prophet

Jeremiah? As He was revealing Jeremiah's calling to him, He touched his mouth.

> Then the LORD put forth his hand and touched my mouth. And the LORD said unto me, Behold, I have put my words in thy mouth.
> —Jeremiah 1:9, KJV

One of the primary places of prophetic government is the mouth of prophets. This is not only true of the office of the prophet but also of the prophetic responsibility of the believer. We are to speak in alignment with heaven's plans. We must be aware of the power in our mouths and the creativity of our words. This is particularly true in dealing with reclaiming ground in a territory. It is easy to yield to the temptation of continually speaking the problem that has long existed in the region. I have seen instances where apostolic leaders become immensely frustrated and discouraged, and they begin to curse the territory they have been appointed to redeem. In doing so, they are revoking the promise of the Lord for their lives and their territory. Not only are they retreating from the will of God, but they are coming into agreement with the will of the enemy—in essence forming a demonic vow that needs to be broken. This is one reason prophetic intercessors, prophetic prayer, governmental intercession, and life-giving prophetic worship are necessary for a region or a territory. A vibrant apostolic hub must create an atmosphere of life and creativity. Remember, in the Book of Genesis God's Spirit was hovering; His voice was residing in the midst of the glory. The creativity of God is housed in the glory of God. The voice of God lives and dwells in the midst of His glory. As we create atmospheres of glory, we open ourselves to receiving the voice of God and to the release of that voice to the region and the territory. As the voice of God and the mind of God are released into the atmosphere, the creative potential and power of God move forward in the territory, thereby completing the work of redemption.

Chapter 6

WORD, WORSHIP, AND PRAYER

The three pillars—the Word, worship, and prayer—are critical in the advancement of the kingdom of God in a region or territory. A strong prevailing preaching ministry blasts demonic powers and releases the Lord's life-giving vision. The profound ministry of teaching releases revelation that fuels personal and corporate transformation. As worship goes up from the apostolic base, it engages the atmosphere in the territory, bringing a much-needed shift and lifting the people into an encounter that will forever change their lives and mark them with hunger. Prayer is an essential ingredient in the work of transformation. The powers of hell will do everything they can to assail the progress of the emerging apostolic hub. This is why a strong base of people must form an apostolic company and together seek the Lord for His will in a region or territory, with unwavering commitment.

WORSHIP AND THE WORD

As kingdom works become established in a region, the apostle must establish a strong foundation of the Word of God. This is paramount in the origination of a substantial apostolic work in the territory. The ministry of preaching and teaching has to be a central focus of the emerging apostolic ministry. Demonic strongholds and systems of thought must be dismantled by the release of a potent declaration of the Word of God. The apostle must also raise his or her fivefold ministry team to renew the minds of the people. The apostolic leader must create an atmosphere of intense confrontation and deliverance, as well as build a house that glorifies and magnifies the name of Jesus and raise radical prophetic worshippers in the lineage of the tabernacle of David. David's tabernacle is a powerful biblical example because it shows us how to fight from a place of glory. As David built a zone of continual prayer and worship, he was creating a throne for the Lord to rest upon.

So he left Asaph and his relatives there before the ark of the covenant of the LORD to minister before the ark continually, as every day's work required; and Obed-edom with his 68 relatives; Obed-edom, also the son of Jeduthun, and Hosah as gatekeepers. He left Zadok the priest and his relatives the priests before the tabernacle of the LORD in the high place which was at Gibeon, to offer burnt offerings to the LORD on the altar of burnt offering continually morning and evening, even according to all that is written in the law of the LORD, which He commanded Israel. With them were Heman and Jeduthun, and the rest who were chosen, who were designated by name, to give thanks to the LORD, because His lovingkindness is everlasting. And with them were Heman and Jeduthun with trumpets and cymbals for those who should sound aloud, and with instruments for the songs of God, and the sons of Jeduthun for the gate.

—1 Chronicles 16:37–42

Under David's rule, Israel enjoyed the blessings of God. It's important to remember how David arrived at the palace. As a rejected young man, he found solace in a place of solitude and intimacy with God. While his brothers seemed to despise him and his father often misunderstood him and relegated him to the tending of sheep, an activity designed for a servant, David pursued God. He was formed in the wilderness as a worshipping warrior. He was a man who possessed great masculinity yet knew how to be tender and broken in the presence of God, something that is often a struggle in the modern church. We have been misinformed if we think that passion and radical adoration worship is a feminine act when in fact many of the Bible's most notable characters were strong men who knew how to fight but also enjoyed the deep place of surrender in God. David was such a man. He was full of love for his Creator and loved to worship God.

David understood the vital role of worship in maintaining his kingship and continuing the blessing of God for the people of Israel. It was with that in mind that he created the tabernacle to honor the ark. He assigned Asaph and a company of minstrels to minister to the Lord continually. Their primary assignment was to maintain the honor and adoration of the presence of God. Asaph was a unique prophetic minstrel who knew how to release the song of the Lord and break through the atmosphere. We need such potent prophetic minstrels in this hour to establish a throne-room atmosphere. Many people think of the throne room as solely a place of worship, but it is in fact the place where the God of the universe sits upon the throne. He rules from an atmosphere of glory, and He has called His children to understand how to rule in the earth amid the glory of God. Worship is an intercessory tool. There is a level of worship and praise that creates a place of habitation where the presence of the Lord dwells amongst His people. It is the indwelling presence of God that assists in the work of reclaiming the ground and transformation.

I still remember when God sent me to open up an apostolic church in a very religious territory. I was teaching and preaching many of these concepts, yet they often seem to fall upon deaf ears, as the people had never heard these types of revelations. There were hungry ones who readily accepted what I was sharing and ran with it, yet the vast majority of people in the territory found these things to be uncommon. This is something leaders will have to wrestle with when assigned to territories and regions that earnestly need their gift yet often do not know how to receive it. It is the mandate of the apostle to begin to call forth a Nehemiah people to help build the walls of the kingdom of God.

As I was laboring in my region and contending for both revival and transformation, God had me traveling to the nations. Apostolic churches and ministries are never confined to a single building, but they are given blueprints for regions, territories, and people groups. Many times, God asks a small apostolic church to do big exploits. Remember, the Scripture says little is much when God is in the midst of it (e.g., Lev. 26:8; John 6:9–13). Never measure the strength of an apostolic anointing by numbers and money alone. I have known many leaders who were skilled marketers and transformational thinkers; therefore, they were able to assemble large groups of people and build ministries that looked very successful from the outside. Yet many of them did not know how to adequately prophesy, preach, and demonstrate the kingdom of God or engage in the work of regional transformation in retaking the ground.

During my time of labor and traveling to the nations, the Lord began to highlight to me the vibrant worship I saw in other countries. He told me to come home and create an atmosphere of radical worship with dancing, praising, shouting, prophesying, and long periods of seeking His face. I realized we were to worship not only for the moment we were in but for the surrounding territory and people. In many ways it was intercessory worship. I had neither heard nor thought of such a concept before. That is the thing about Jesus—He will challenge your thinking. As you partner with heaven and gain the insight of the Lord, you will learn new things. I told my people that we were going to create a unique atmosphere of worship. I preached on digging the wells of revival and transformation, and I told the people I was looking for well diggers who would come to the front during every gathering to dance, cry, weep, travail, and pray for an atmosphere of revival. We were not only worshipping for that particular gathering, but we were worshipping for the transformation of a region. Just as David established a tabernacle, we were endeavoring to establish a tabernacle of worship and praise. It was far more than just feelings or momentary experiences—the mandate was lasting transformation.

Many in my church began to catch the vision and partner with digging the wells. Our gatherings started to take on a new vibrancy in the spirit. Yet it was not without conflict, which is one thing every apostolic leader must deal with. There will always be resistance to new concepts and revelations. The region I was in was one bound by the spirit of religion, and the voice of worship was muted. There was little to no understanding of prophetic worship, much less ground-shaking praise. Yet I was determined because I had heard the voice of God. I did my best to cultivate a strong prophetic worship team that knew not only to navigate atmospheres but to shift them and create new ones. I preached and preached again the necessity of prophetic worship to our church. Some people got angry at the direction we were going in and left, but I was undeterred. I knew I'd heard from heaven, and I knew we were to establish a throne-room atmosphere. Over time we began to see significant breakthroughs in the territory. Each little victory was one we labored hard for, but it was worth it as we saw lives changed and the atmosphere shifting. Worship is a vital tool in reclaiming ground.

PRAYER AND POWER

Intercessory prayer is also a critical element in reclaiming the ground in a region.

> On your walls, O Jerusalem, I have appointed watchmen; all day and all night they will never keep silent. You who remind the LORD, take no rest for yourselves; and give Him no rest until He establishes and makes Jerusalem a praise in the earth.
>
> —Isaiah 62:6–7

There must be a praying spirit amongst people who have committed to territorial transformation. Let's remember it was prayer that fueled the move of God in the early church. The Lord Jesus said His house was to be called a house of prayer (Matt. 21:13). If we measured many churches in our current culture by this standard, they would fail. It is impossible to have intimacy with Jesus without a healthy prayer life. Prayer is divided into many categories, spanning from personal intimacy to corporate agreement and far beyond. For the sake of this writing, we will focus primarily on intercession.

Intercession begins with a burden. A quick study of every great work committed to the hands of men by God will reveal a point in which God transferred a burden to the spirit of a man or woman. There was something in the heart of God that was divinely released into the heart of one of His children. As His child took that burden, it led him or her to a place of communication with God to co-labor with Him in giving birth to something designed to shift the lives and destinies of others. In the ministry of intercession we stand between life and death and between the power of heaven and hell; we stand in the gap for the destiny of other human beings. Rather than relegating their destiny to chance or human persuasion, we determine in our hearts to plead our case in the courtroom of heaven. We do such in the holiest sense through a sovereign burden released into our hearts by the Creator of the universe.

Intercession can be laborious at times, but it brings unquenchable joy when answered prayer erupts forth. Intercession may begin with a burden, but it continues because of faith in the heart of a person who chooses to contradict natural circumstances and demonic accusations and instead boldly stand on the Word of God. When a corporate group begins to intercede for a region and its citizens, they loose the eternal power of heaven itself, moving from the unseen realm into the seen realm by the spirit of faith. They engage demon rulers traversing the second heaven and bind them with authority.

One of the most dramatic Scripture passages that relates to intercessory prayer is in the Gospel of Matthew.

> I will give you the keys (authority) of the kingdom of heaven; and whatever you bind [forbid, declare to be improper and unlawful] on earth will have [already] been bound in heaven, and whatever you loose [permit, declare lawful] on earth will have [already] been loosed in heaven.
> —Matthew 16:19, AMP

I call this kind of intercession *governmental prayer*. You may ask, What does it mean to govern? I would simply say it means to legislate. Jesus instructed us to exercise the authority to bind and to loose, to declare lawful or unlawful. We began this teaching looking at and pondering the question of what God's dream is for people in a place. To properly realize that dream, we have to engage in a daring art called intercessory prayer. An apostolic group of people must know how to combat the evil forces looking to oppose the work of God in a territory. While bridal intimacy is a form of prayer and worship in which our hearts beat with passion toward our Bridegroom, it is only one portion of the miraculous work of prayer. There is another portion that is remarkably integrated into the work of intercession—governmental prayer. It is a form of prayer in which we boldly stand upon the prophecies of the Lord, the written promises of God, and the utterances given to us in the secret place, and we forbid unlawful the operations of hell. We use our authority as gatekeepers and sons and daughters of the living God to loose the power and the glory of heaven. We call upon the name of Jesus and all of His majesty to sweep through a region and a territory, releasing blessing, redemption, salvation, healing, and restoration.

A strong prayer team is critical in an apostolic hub. They cannot pray for their agenda or their desire. They must come under the authority of the set leader and the leadership team. Often when you get a prayer group going, the spirit of Jezebel and other forces will try to infiltrate to derail the work of God. The enemy understands that intercessory prayer is the engine of a spiritual house. Without the engine of prayer being revved up and maintained with fresh fuel, the house will begin to stagnate and move backward in the agenda of the Lord. The intercessors must have prophetic people and prophets in their midst to discern attacks and release key prophetic words. Those words should be both reviewed and judged by the leaders of the house to make sure they are in line with what God is speaking to the set team.

Proper training is critical in the work of intercessory prayer. This is where the ministry of teaching is so important. Not only does there need to be strong intercessory teams, but the people in the ministry need to take on a spirit of prayer—and not just intercessory prayer but prayer in all of its glorious facets.

Reclaiming the ground in a territory or region is an apostolic concept. It is one of the mandates of true apostles. It is a multi-pronged strategy that begins with a strong call from God, the establishment of a vibrant apostolic company, and the continued commitment to transformation. The regional rulers will have to be uncovered. Sound and biblically based spiritual warfare strategies will need to be engaged. The corporate power of the ekklesia will need to be implemented. One-on-one deliverance will need to be done. The full fivefold ministry gifts will need to be released. A vibrant people of prayer will need to be established along with worship, as we've already discussed.

I love the example given by a great revivalist in our generation as he compared a church to a greenhouse. He painted the picture of a place where vegetation would grow unrestricted by the atmosphere outside of it.[3] In many ways I think this is a picture of an apostolic church. Despite the atmosphere all around it, people are established in a place where the fullness of the kingdom of God is enlarged and expanded. When we think of the concept of reclaiming the ground, we must realize that even in the times of the Bible, there were groups of people who would not align their hearts with Jesus. While I believe the power of God can transform entire cities, I also think that many times ground taking will begin with a group of people who decide to come out from under the influence of the ruling spirit. Collectively they form an atmosphere—like a greenhouse—where they begin to grow and flourish in the glory of God. They establish a strong apostolic hub that serves as a base for the move of God in the territory. Even though portions of the territory never fully align with the plan of God, they reclaim their assigned ground with epic results in the lives of the people and the region surrounding them.

Sometimes as we endeavor to believe God for the shifting of territory, we can become discouraged by what we deem to be a lack of progress. We must recognize the house of the Lord and the people of God form a canopy within the region that provides refuge, protection, and a place to experience the ultimate blessings of God. A strong apostolic leader recognizes the greatest shift will be in the hearts of the people they lead, both on an individual and corporate level. I believe Scripture is clear that we can and should believe for the corporate destiny of a people group in a region, but I also recognize that some will ultimately choose the way of the enemy and refuse to yield their hearts to the plan of God. I cannot overemphasize how critical it is that the apostolic leader doesn't base his or her account of success on the totality of events within their region. Yes, a governing ministry will influence the area, but it also creates a strong base of operations. That apostolic base does not need to be judged simply by numbers and finances but by the level of transformation happening in the lives of people. An examination of church history reveals that quite often great things happen with a small group of people. God chooses unlikely candidates to do exploits.

A strong apostolic hub forms a stronghold of faith. We often talk about negative strongholds, but we fail to recognize there are positive ones. A stronghold is a fortified place, a city with walls all around it. God uses the apostolic hub as a kingdom stronghold. The leadership team fortifies the walls with the revelation of faith and apostolic authority. They release governing sounds, decrees, and teaching. They pray and govern the shifting atmosphere in the space they are located. This, in and of itself, is a work of transformation. Leaders must not yield to the weight of discouragement simply because God has put a desire for even more in their hearts. They must recognize that transformation begins at home.

> But ye shall receive power, after that the Holy Ghost is come upon you: and ye shall be witnesses unto me both in Jerusalem, and in all Judaea, and in Samaria, and unto the uttermost part of the earth.
> —Acts 1:8, KJV

While the verse in Acts is speaking specifically about the outpouring of the Holy Spirit, I believe there's an application here that fits with our current conversation. The move of God first begins on the local level. It then expands out to the surrounding region, then the nation, and finally other nations. I call this apostolic influence and progression. The apostolic anointing is not one that is boxed in. It is an anointing that breaks barriers and walls to reach far beyond any limitations. It begins transformation by impacting and equipping the people God sends to become a part of the work. It then labors to establish a greenhouse that shelters the people of God from the demonic rulers in the region and territory and gives them a safe space to renew their minds and come out from under the influence of oppression. As it gains strength in the territory, it will expand and advance its reach until it eventually has a strong voice throughout the region. Does that mean that every single person or even the majority of people will buy into what Jesus is speaking over the territory? In cases of mass revival, the answer is yes. But there are cases in which the answer is no. The gospel must go forth regardless of the response of human beings. The fact that there is a strong apostolic leader in the region for the work of transformation is a testimony of the faithfulness of God. It does not matter if people choose not to surrender to the will of God and the mandate of the apostle in the territory. God's work will still go forward, and there will be a substantial house of glory that will reach the hungry people.

So just to recap: God provides a mandate for a region or territory that is apostolic. Apostles go under the mandate of heaven. They labor to establish a work and an apostolic company. Over a period of time, the work and the people gain strength in the region while ripping apart the demonic architecture and building a kingdom structure. As God blesses their work, it grows to the size and stature that God ordains and that the people are willing to partner with. Over time the work will hopefully gain a strong foothold in the territory with results far beyond the work itself. In cases of awakening and revival, the entire territory can be shaken by the glory of God, but it begins with small steps and continues with diligent labor. As the Apostle Paul so eloquently stated, each of us is nothing more than a planter in the kingdom of God who is responsible to plant seeds. Others will water them, but it is God who gives the increase.

> I planted, Apollos watered, but God was causing the growth. So then neither the one who plants nor the one who waters is anything, but God who causes the growth. Now he who plants and he who waters are one; but each will receive his own reward according to his own labor. For we are God's fellow workers; you are God's field, God's building.
> —1 Corinthians 3:6–9

We must relinquish control over the size and scope of our work for the Lord or the work to which we are attached. We must not be consumed with personal or corporate ambition. Instead we must consecrate our desires and lay them on the altar of the Lord for Him to breathe upon and expand as He sees fit. Our assignment is to remain committed to the vision and faithful to surrender, while trusting God to provide the increase.

Chapter 7

TENDING YOUR OWN SOIL

Now let's talk about reclaiming ground in your own heart. We have sufficiently made a case for believing God to take ground in territories, but what about the ground in your own life? The seeds of greatness can't grow and flourish if the ground of your heart is stony and filled with weeds. This will abort the work of the kingdom in your life personally and will manifest when you participate in an apostolic company with the mandate to bring transformation to a sphere or physical place. All too often, unresolved wounds resurface in the midst of spiritual battles.

God, as a loving Father, will reveal the heart issues and provide grace to overcome.

HEALING AND WHOLENESS

When the Holy Spirit highlights areas of your own heart that need to be resolved and healed, it is an opportunity to apply the healing power of God. This is a personal responsibility that is vital to be effective in the kingdom of God. Many people are fighting spiritual battles that are the result of an untended garden in their hearts. They have not taken the personal responsibility of stewardship seriously. They have not intentionally dug deep into the Word of God to find the scriptural foundation to renew their minds, eradicate mental warfare and bondage, and gain ground over the enemy. I believe the Lord is drawing you to a strong place of healing and provision.

> GOD, my shepherd! I don't need a thing. You have bedded me down in lush meadows, you find me quiet pools to drink from. True to your word, you let me catch my breath and send me in the right direction.
>
> —Psalm 23:1–3, MSG

I love Psalm 23. Jesus reveals himself as the Great Shepherd. One of the responsibilities of the Shepherd is the protection and health of the sheep. In the opening verses the Lord reveals His role in our lives as a provider. This is one of the concepts that the spirit of religion aggressively goes after. The spirit of religion hates believers coming into alignment with their identity in God. The promises of God in the New Testament show that our salvation covers identity. We are no longer strangers, orphans, or rejected, but we are abundantly accepted in the Beloved through the extraordinary sacrifice of Jesus Christ (Eph. 1:3–8). The realization and acceptance of this truth set us free from shame and bondage.

The Great Shepherd leads us to a place that is both peaceful and rich in abundance. How can you be at peace when your mind is being harassed and tormented? The answer is simple: you cannot. One of the mandates of Jesus in your life is to lead you down a pathway of complete emotional healing. This means the uprooting of seeds of trauma, fear, pain, and rejection. As you journey hand in hand with Jesus into the walk of the Spirit, you move from pain to prosperity. You advance from fear to faith. You exit abandonment, and you enter acceptance. Not only has the Father provided love and acceptance for you, but Jesus also shed His blood to secure your place in the family of God.

As if that were not enough, God sent the Holy Spirit into the earth to take up full-time residency in the hearts of born-again men and women. He serves as a teacher, intercessor, and revealer. When you yield yourself to the life-giving walk of the Spirit, you engage the Holy Spirit as an active participant in your renewal and redemption. Daily He illuminates truth to your mind—truth that holds the answers to eradicate death and bondage. As you consistently spend time praying in the Spirit, worshipping God, and meditating on His Word, you release rivers of redemption and freedom in your life.

Tending the garden of your soul is not a life of toil and hard labor. It is the result of a life-giving journey and partnership with God. You come up higher in your understanding of your thinking. You exit the limitation of human thought and break through the lid of your incapability. You soar with God as you come to understand He is the greatest thinker in all of creation, and He has invited you into the expanse of His all-encompassing genius. You have the opportunity to abandon a pathway of fearful thinking and anxious living to receive mercy, grace, and strength from heaven.

I believe one of the things the Lord wants to do is bring you personally into a place of radical transformation and change. He desires to get you into a place of powerful kingdom function, free from past struggles and bondage. Often children of God are struggling with the sins of previous generations and strongholds in their own families, yet I believe there's a place of absolute freedom that Jesus paid the ultimate price for. He did not pay the price so you could be partially free. In fact, when He was on the cross, He boldly declared it is finished (John 19:30). You must recognize that Jesus provided complete wholeness for you. You must have a vision for your life that includes total freedom.

WHAT ARE YOU SOWING?

Every day of your life, seeds are being planted in the garden of your heart. The entire revelation of the kingdom can be summed up in the concept of seedtime and harvest. Everything begins as a seed. The realization of the power of sowing is a vital kingdom concept. Mature believers understand the need to guard their hearts while sowing the right seeds, watering those seeds, and creating an atmosphere in their lives ripe for harvest. In the Book of Jeremiah the Lord compares our lives and our hearts to a garden.

> They will come and shout for joy on the height of Zion, and they will be radiant over the bounty of the Lord—over the grain and the new wine

and the oil, and over the young of the flock and the herd; and their life will be like a watered garden, and they will never languish again.

—Jeremiah 31:12

The question is, What seeds are you sowing?

In the parable of the sower Jesus said your heart is like soil. You are charged with the responsibility of planting the right seeds and nurturing them. Diligent stewardship will bring abundant rewards to your life. The Bible declares that you will bring forth good fruit, some thirty, some sixty, and some a hundredfold (Matt. 13:23). According to obedience and stewardship, various people will produce different levels of fruit in their lives.

Yet the seed remains the same! It is the life-giving Word of God. It is the Spirit and the truth declared in God's Word. Each word, each story, each revelation contains the power to establish, build, and deliver. As you dive deep into the Word of God, you unlock His mind for your life. You tap the power of divine transformation. You release the unfailing strength of God's Word. I believe one of the primary factors determining how much you produce is the condition of your heart. What type of soil have you cultivated? Is there ground that is filled with bitterness? Is there toxicity from unresolved wounds? Have you tended the ground and prepared it for the seed?

You must prepare your heart for the seed of the Word of God. In many cases you have to reclaim the ground from past traumas, generational bondages, bloodline curses, and painful experiences. There is power in the name of Jesus and in prayer to bring much-needed transformation. Utilizing the tools of the armor of God, the blood of Jesus, and the power of His name can be critical in preparing the ground of your heart for expansion and enlargement.

> Keep [or guard] your heart with all diligence,
> for out of it spring the issues of life.
> — Proverbs 4:23, NKJV

Your heart in this context speaks of the place in your mind where your conscience is housed. One of the most challenging issues with past trauma is the effects that can linger in your mind. Yet Jesus said, "Let this mind be in you which was also in Christ Jesus" (Phil. 2:5, NKJV). We are also told in the Book of Romans that we can renew our minds (12:2). The Word of God is like medicine that can heal the deepest recesses of the human mind, collecting all the pain and the emotional scarring and removing it. Proper study of, application of, and meditation on the Word of God is a healing instrument for the heart of man.

As you reclaim ground in your inner man—in your mind, will, and emotions—you must begin to recognize impure thought patterns. You have the authority of the name of Jesus to cast those thoughts down. You also can apply the Word of God to those areas of your thought life. This is often a long-term process that demands commitment. Many people get frustrated and discouraged when they don't see overnight change. While I believe in instant deliverance and radical miracles, I also believe that there are often things in our lives that must be changed through a process. It's OK to be in the process of reformation in your personal life. The grace of God is there—even when you blow it, He lovingly picks you up and assists you in getting back on track.

As you are guarding your heart, you are also using your faith to move mountains in your emotional life. This means when you begin to see old cycles of rejection and pain resurfacing, you must be quick to break those things in the name of Jesus. This is part of the deliverance process as you reclaim the ground in your thought life.

The entire mission of Jesus was to seek and save the lost (Luke 19:10). It is with that in mind that you can look forward to reclaiming the ground in your life. For the Lord to send you forth into the midst of a hurting world to preach the gospel of

Jesus Christ with boldness, authenticity, and sincerity, you must start by reclaiming the ground in your own life and heart. Then it's time to reclaim the ground in your family, your city, your region, and your nation.

It's time to prepare the soil of your heart and your community to receive the seed of the Word of God. It's time to loosen up the hard ground and stony places in your own heart and allow the tenderness of the Lord to manifest in your life. It's time to cast out every hidden demon. It's time to speak to the mountain and command the mountain to move. It's time to release the power of Spirit-filled worship in your home and your life. It's time to arise to higher and greater levels of service to King Jesus.

Chapter 8

CONCLUSION

As I read the pages of the Book of Acts, I'm inspired by the ability of God to take a radical band of misfits and use them to turn the world upside down.

> But when they did not find them, they dragged Jason and some brethren to the rulers of the city, crying out, "These who have turned the world upside down have come here too."
>
> —Acts 17:6, NKJV

The early church apostles were known as those who had turned the world upside down. They moved beyond the limits of natural government as ambassadors of a present and working kingdom in the earth. They manifested the power of the gospel, with signs and wonders following. They plowed ground that was hard and seemingly locked up to release revival over territories. They preached messages that angered the religious, motivating them to persecute the burgeoning church severely. Yet despite their bonds and afflictions they continued to follow Jesus with unparalleled passion. As they honored Him and His name in the earth, He confirmed and validated their ministries with supernatural multiplication. The Book of Acts is the story of exploits with and in God. He masterfully chose seemingly average men and women to do extraordinary things on the earth. The only limit they had was in their minds with their inability to believe in the power of God.

Where are today's world shakers? Where are those who will dare to dream with God? Where are those who will believe God for cities, regions, and nations? Where are those who will believe God to conquer the mountains of society? Where are those who are willing to make their mark on society in a way nobody expected?

There is a strong and bold apostolic call going out to the nations of the world. The Lord of all glory is asking, "Who can I send? Who is ready to go for Me?" I pray your answer will be,

CONCLUSION

"Here am I, Lord. Send me!" (See Isaiah 6:8–9.) To go forth with great power, the ground of your life must be prepared. I pray that as you've read the words in this writing, you have allowed the Holy Spirit to minister to you in a deep, profound way, giving you a vision for a new level of healing and deliverance. I'm asking the Lord today to surround you with His glory, His grace, and His power. I'm asking for a fresh and tangible release of the healing power of God over your life, in the name of Jesus.

I believe that the heart of God is beating for nations and territories. The critical question is, What is Your dream for us, Lord? Heaven is inviting us into the greatest adventure of our lives—to dream with God. We are to take Him by the hand and walk boldly into the unknown on a mission to please our Father. He is opening up places and spaces for us to reclaim for fruitfulness in His kingdom. The time is now, the mandate is here, and the power is available. **Let's go!**

NOTES

[1] *Merriam-Webster*, s.v. "perspective," accessed September 28, 2020, https://www.merriam-webster.com/dictionary/perspective.

[2] Blue Letter Bible, s.v. "*legiōn*," accessed September 29, 2020, https://www.blueletterbible.org/lang/lexicon/lexicon.cfm?Strongs=G3003&t=NKJV.

[3] Bill Johnson, *The Way of Life: Experiencing the Culture of Heaven on Earth* (Shippensburg, PA: Destiny Image, 2018), 30, https://www.amazon.com/Way-Life-Experiencing-Culture-Heaven/dp/0768442729.